From Earth's Floor

From Earth's Floor

Small Poems

MARIANNA BUSCHING

RESOURCE *Publications* • Eugene, Oregon

FROM EARTH'S FLOOR
Small Poems

Copyright © 2025 Marianna Busching. All rights reserved. Except for brief quotations in critical publications or reviews, no part of this book may be reproduced in any manner without prior written permission from the publisher. Write: Permissions, Wipf and Stock Publishers, 199 W. 8th Ave., Suite 3, Eugene, OR 97401.

Resource Publications
An Imprint of Wipf and Stock Publishers
199 W. 8th Ave., Suite 3
Eugene, OR 97401

www.wipfandstock.com

PAPERBACK ISBN: 979-8-3852-6357-8
HARDCOVER ISBN: 979-8-3852-6358-5
EBOOK ISBN: 979-8-3852-6359-2
VERSION NUMBER 11/25/25

To my brother Dale

"Where were you when I laid the foundations of the earth?
... On what were its bases sunk, or who laid its cornerstone when the morning stars sang together and all the heavenly beings shouted for joy?"

Job 38:4a, 6, 7

Contents

Acknowledgments | ix

Wonder and Doubt

To One Who Is Losing His Faith | 3
From Earth's Floor | 4
South African Eucharist | 6
Madonnas: A Painting | 7
Supper | 8

Prayers

Prayer for My Legs | 11
Prayer for a Late Day | 12
Thanks for Small Discomforts | 14
Prayer in Depression | 16
The Answer | 17
Rant and Litany | 19

Holy Days

Annunciation | 23
The Size of Love | 25
Carol for Christmas Eve | 26
Good Friday | 27
Fasting on Good Friday | 28
Sunrise in Hell | 29
Easter | 30
It Must Have Been Love | 31

Seraphic Beings

To See an Angel | 35
If I Could Imagine Gabriel | 36
Angels | 37
A Fantasy of Ending the War | 38

Beginnings and Endings

In the Kitchen of Creation | 41
When God Began | 42
Somehow | 43
Shiny Things | 44
A Dream of the Afterlife | 45
Last Lent | 47

Acknowledgments

First of all, I'd like to thank my husband Joe Mainolfi, who generously gave me the time to work on this project and to write and *write*. I also want to thank my sponsors: The Very Reverend Rob Boulter, Dean of the Cathedral of the Incarnation in Baltimore; The Reverend Ann Copp, a teacher of Western civilization and an ordained Episcopalian priest, now retired; and my dear teacher and mentor, Mary Azrael, who, in her poetry class at Johns Hopkins University, taught me to craft anything from sonnets to pantoums, and who gave me great and constant encouragement.

I also want to thank my beta reader, Rachel Hicks, who is herself an editor and a published poet, for her careful reading and fine, helpful suggestions. I am especially honored to thank my daughter, Sharon Doyle, who contributed the photos in this chapbook. Special thanks to my son-in-law Ronnie Doyle who helped me with the vocabulary and the vagaries of the computer.

My acknowledgments also of the journals and magazines that published the following poems:

"Supper"—Published in *The Living Church* and in *Time of Singing*

"Rant and Litany"—First Place Winner of the Virginia Poetry Society Competition

"Carol for Christmas Eve"—Published in *Ancient Paths*

"Easter"—Published twice in *The Bible Advocate*

"To See an Angel"—Published in *Inspirit*

"If I Could Imagine Gabriel"—Published in *Tickled by Thunder*

"A Fantasy of Ending the War"—Published in *Transcendent Visions*

"In the Kitchen of Creation"—Published in *Leading Edge Magazine*

"Shiny Things"—Published in *Across the Long Bridge*

Wonder and Doubt

To One Who Is Losing His Faith

It really doesn't matter
whether you fall on impious knees
and your heretical thoughts scatter
in broken prayers. If Faith flees,
dancing off in Reason's arms,
busily counting errors and deaths,
you're only hearing bleak alarms
of buried questions. The breaths
you take are mysterious fuel. You move
with inner electricity during the decades
of your heartbeat. What distant Love
ignited you? When faith fades,
reflect on life's wonder. That might
be called Worship, holier than
ancient rituals. Those midnight
doubts but prove a man
is wrestling with a Power
that eons can't erase
and in some secret, predawn hour,
may meet Him face to Face.

From Earth's Floor

Walking here on earth's floor,
feet in fallen twigs,
I look for signs.
Microbes, stars, furred mammals,
stone mollusks
don't seem to be enough.

I want to feel the grainy
hand of the Creator, broad
with its millennia of muscle.
I want to feel His palm
under me so that,
worshipping, I am carried
like an apple and set shining
on His table.

I want to sing, face to Face,
His praises in my highest,
most luminous notes.

I want to offer Him
my questions: Why
are we alone? What

is death? Where
has He been these many
thousand years?
He doesn't have to answer yet.
I can wait.

South African Eucharist

This latter-day Eden
is brittle grass and
flat, dangerous trees.
Pools edged with crackled mud
shine shallow and green.
The red earth offers scattered stones
to the biting sun.
This is where creatures
with tough pelts and leather skin
leap or tread ponderously.

No human belongs here.
Having named them all,
Oh! that man might withdraw,
leaving the beasts in their peculiar majesty,
to their innocent drinking
of each other's blood,
the ordained eating
of the other's flesh.

It is their necessary worship
after the Fall.

Madonnas: A Painting

Mute five hundred years
behind shimmering brushstrokes,
we flatten our milky breasts
with long, pious hands,
our faces alight with slight
frozen smiles. Lapis-blue veils
slip sideways over our hair. We
can't adjust them. Cherubs hang
motionless, silent songs
gathered in their mouths.
We will never hear their harmonies
or smell the rose garlands woven
among the trees.

A cross
stands in the greenish sky
behind our shoulders.
We can't strike out in sorrow
or weep or even kiss
the Baby's haloed head.
Our full, pearly eyelids are lowered,
avoiding the probing glance
of God.

Supper

What sweet logic that He,
the Incorruptible, should feed us bread
and call it body! For surely,
it is. What flesh could wrap
a Spirit such as His except
the very fabric of life,
its rich grains fused
with fragrant golden heat?
And what could sing along celestial veins
except the exuberant wine?
Press the bread into our hands.
Lift the cup to all our lips.
The Mystery is so deep,
it's no mystery at all.

Prayers

Prayer for My Legs

Lord, for these stout legs,
strong and unloved,
their sturdy peasant plainness
purposely covered and hidden,
I ask that their trusted, ignored muscles
not waver into reluctance,
not topple into weakness.

Forgive my dismissal
of their tireless steel,
their seven decades
of uncomplaining labor
that carried me swiftly upright
painless on oiled joints
over carpets and stairs,
rocks, snow-deep fields,
forest floors.
I love them now, Lord,
those unbeautiful servants.
Bless and keep them.

Prayer for a Late Day

When those microscopic doors
behind my eyes begin to close,
and I can no longer find the latch,
Lord, let some gates stand open:

A bed standing in sunset light,
my baby son like a soft
fragrant peach in my curved arm;
a walk with my brother
on a hot thundery day
with no boundaries on our words;
the moment I gazed upon a summer forest
and first understood that I will go
and it will stay;
a bedroom window standing open
to the blossoming birdsong morning
and my beloved beside me.

Let some path lead back into those gardens,
Lord, some light remain aflame.
When the dimness approaches,
lead me into remembered heavens
that if I wait here,

I might linger in joy.
For Thy mercy's sake.

Thanks for Small Discomforts

Knee, too many
squats at the gym yesterday?
Do you remember, Stomach,
what is making you complain
to my belt?

I see a slight salty swelling
in my foot. Bunion,
are you quarreling
with my shoe again?
Cornea, why are you thirsty?
Too much wind today?

A crack in my back
warns me: Sorry. This might be
a restless night.
When I rise from my chair,
leg joints click tiny castanets.
This is not a samba,
I gently reprimand.

Nose, why must you
be wiped again? Bladder,

I feel you filling up.
Good work! What is a short walk
down the hall, after all?
I give thanks for these small discomforts
because they are small.

Prayer in Depression

Let me not despise myself.
Release me from this locked, dusty room
where I count my sins
like dirty pebbles, stacking them
in a dark and earthen corner.
Free me from this worn circle of regret
that I tread like a yoked animal.
Water again my desiccated heart.
Open the windows of my soul
and teach me the forgotten craft
of joy.

The Answer

(My Son Prays)

One night, praying alone,
you sweated on your knees beside the bed,
pleading for hours:
"Should I go or should I stay?"

And at last you heard the answer arrive.
You heard it with your cells,
with your ears,
clear words in English
scrolling through your brain
like the stock market index.
You shook with surprise
and the shock of disbelief.

It was the first and only time
God spoke to you,
and they were words
you didn't expect
or even wanted to hear:

"Happiness lies in the presence
of the Lord."

You took your family,
left California
and returned to the Midwest.
And happiness followed.

Rant and Litany

(Upon the Death of My Father)

Great liar! whose wings have fallen
pearl after pearl feather scorching,
curling black in acrid, smoking spikes,
what have you concocted?
What imagined revenge have you taken
upon the eternal I-Will-Be-What-I-Will-Be?
You hoofed monster! You invented rot,
you crafted corruption, you learned
how to stop breath, how to turn sacred dust
into ordinary dirt, unlabeled and forgotten.
You took the whole of green
and gold creation and made it temporary.
The perfect galaxies wobble
on their axis. Caverns ignite.
Spheres explode.
You discovered chaos and turned it loose.

Flail and gnash, fiery reptile . . .
I sneer at your impotence.
Offer bribes, malformed demon . . .
My ransom has been paid.
Frighten me with the pit, evil stench . . .

My mansion stands among the stars.
Delude yourself with wars, bloody destroyer . . .
The Victory has been won.
Threaten me with extinction, ravenous executioner . . .
The Holy One has taken my place
and death is but a door.

Holy Days

Annunciation

We think we know almost
as much as God with our screens, their instant knowledge
fed easily to us.

Yet every Christmas we expect the Child,
as Mary did not
when she was flooded
in the stunning sunrays
of the messenger.

In chilled twilight we prepare the crib, the straw;
we are the innkeeper.

Stringing lights on doorways,
we are the star.

Singing carols,
we are the angels.

Alone at night with clasped hands
we are the shepherds, amazed.

With tumbles of gleaming gifts
we are the Magi.

Seated before our glowing
blue screens,
we feel we know almost
as much as God.

But every year,
we wait for Him.

The Size of Love

How simple, small and narrow . . .
straw-sweet yet odorous as though
foretelling deathly sorrow
the manger stands in glow
of sooty, guttered firelight,
while above the darkened fields, wings
of radiant beings beat a flight
of song that all of heaven sings.
So small and so contained
on an unswept bit of earth,
emerging human from the holy pain
of that mysterious birth. . . .
So simple and so small
lies the Creator of us all.

Carol for Christmas Eve

O Brightness rocketing from starry dark,
Igniter of life's leaping spark,
O Yearning Power, alone, apart,
creating children for His heart,
O Deliverer, O Sacrifice,
O Universe shrunk to human size,

receive us at your feedstall bed,
crude noble creatures at your head;
guide us through the desert night
to skies dissolved in singing light.
Take folded hands and humbled knee
as on this eve we worship Thee.

Good Friday

Bless my labor today
carried on in mundane routine.
Would that two thousand years ago
I'd have shivered beneath
your bleeding feet, all tasks
forgotten save that of weeping.

But now I know Easter,
the thunder of angelic power
and your glowing absence
from the cave.
I've suspected celestial negotiations,
heavenly compromises:
"Yes, they may suffer, they may die,
but at the end of time
My children are Mine."

Bless my ordinary tasks today
as I think on Thee.

Fasting on Good Friday

Today I cannot share with you
any suffering. What paltry
hunger pangs for a single day
without food! I am thick
and strong, lying
on cushions in sunlight.
I feel I need forgiveness
even for my meditation.

But accept my plea
that when it becomes my
turn to suffer excruciating
attempts to live,
you will lift my pain,
though I couldn't share yours.
Together we will rise
to radiant life

leaving Death behind,
his arms sagging with
discarded torment.

Sunrise in Hell

(from a painting by the same name
in a cathedral in Florence, Italy)

On white coals, on charred feet
whose bone-deep blisters eternally repeat
their agony, stand eons of souls.
Their hoarse, repentant, hopeless cries
shriek from ashy mouths. Their eyes,
long melted, gape with blackened holes
to smoky ceilings. Their hands drip flames.
But that third day, He calls their names,
He treads their scalding paths. With cool
hands, He pours a blessed pool,
a sweet Bethesda, placid, blue.
The condemned, weeping, rise with new
and perfect limbs, kneel at the cloud
that, radiant, hides the throne of God.

Easter

In the meadow lies resurrection,
flat as the water four inches down.
No hot explosion of angels here,
sitting on a smoldering stone,
just lowly mushrooms,
grasses and gray beetles,
acorns rooting under damp leaves,
everything brown and dead yellow,
yet breathing as the earth
rolls in its sleep towards April,
towards endless resurrections
and His promise of our own.

It Must Have Been Love

(Emmaus)

If He unzipped the layered molecules
with their shrieking nerves and salty fluids
to step out of His core of sun-blaze
so that even the resurrection angel
covered his eyes before laying
his scorching hand upon the stone,

then why did He slide back? . . .
back into that dusty leather, subject to gravity
and the ache of gravel under His feet?
Why did He leave open those torn capillaries,
the leaking slit under His ribs?
For ten frightened people?
For one shocked man
with a trembling finger?

Seraphic Beings

To See an Angel

How desperately I want to see
an angel, as described in holy books,
or painted gold on parchment.

To see one appear . . . suddenly, silently
this side of a closed door,
sunrays leaping off him
and his face hidden in radiance,
my heart might explode for joy.
I would think, It's true! They're here!
crowding the transparent air,
their brilliant feet a few inches
above the floor.
I would sink to my knees,
my skin burning in the light,
and wait for their music.

But I've been told
they are messengers, and the news
might not be good.
Or perhaps an old and dear friend,
walking quietly beside me,
has always been
one of them.

If I Could Imagine Gabriel

If I could imagine Gabriel,
his great ankle towering
above my house,
his robes like columns of light
among the pines,
its hem brushing my face
as I stepped off my porch . . .
    and his perfume! Rain
    and lemons and cedar . . .

if I could see
his golden head wreathed
with the sun's firestorms,
and his tall and starry trumpet
braced quietly
near the bus stop,

then I,
at midnight and alone,
would not be afraid.

Angels

They are rife in my house,
in stone, in paint, framed in gilt,
a plastic nightlight, needlepoint cushions,
an amethyst pendant, a pale
ceramic frieze, planted in wreaths,
hanging crystal-brilliant in a window,
climbing a glass candlestick,
molded paper with spread wings
and china face on a shelf
above my head,
faint images of the radiant beings who
with lightning faces and glowing feet
stand invisible
just inside my door.

A Fantasy of Ending the War

An explosion of angels
dripping peach and silver fire
might cause a chain of hands
to clasp in terror across the sands.
In the hot, perfumed wind of blazing wings
and in the powerful harmonies
of brazen trumpets,
who would look to see
whose hand he held?

In the fearful joy
of the blinding, holy light,
they would wrap each other's faces
in their own scarves,
singing the prayers they knew.

Beginnings and Endings

In the Kitchen of Creation

(To Cammie)

In the Creator's sublime kitchen,
ions and atoms are stirred
in pots of copper and clay.
Electric arcs boil and bubble
with a smell of acid and burning oil.
Suns spit and sizzle,
galaxies spread out
like pancakes. On a slab
of space, holes open into
endless dark, like cheese.
Towers of turquoise steam
pop with stars.
Worlds are served up frozen,
smoked, scorched to diamonds
or ringed sour as pickles.

As a dessert
comes the blue, cloud-flavored Earth.

When God Began

When God began the human face,
He did one side first:
glassy eye, waxen ear,
one nostril and a wide, moist mouth.
He smoothed the forehead
with a holy spade,
nudged out half a chin.
Sixteen teeth, he thought,
would be quite lovely.

Stepping back, he wondered
what to do with that slick,
flat side. He pulled, prodded,
popped in one more eye, expanded
the nose with a second damp nostril,
and pinned on another ear.
They were hard to sculpt,
and he was proud.
But the mouth . . . the mouth.
He added sixteen teeth
and a treacherous tongue.
And one of those, he decided,
was more than enough.

Somehow

Somehow
into this first virginal place,
safely locked within crystal walls,
where the two danced every sunrise
and would fly at ease on the wind
among the fruit trees,
their pure bodies entwined,
somehow
into this starry orchard
where flickering pines plucked
their needles like harps,
where great spotted golden cats
would leap to their caresses;
somehow
between the roses
on their smooth, thornless stems,
coiled the reptile.

Shiny Things

Eve loved shiny things. Adam's eyes
beguiled her for hours. The jaguar's fur
was sweeter to stroke than to watch filigreed skies.
The very gate was glittering, set with clear
crystals, flashing carmine at sunrise, blue
at evening when He, fragrant and blinding bright,
walked smiling among the fireflies and threw
stars up and sideways for their delight.
Moons swam in a cherry skin,
pomegranates spilled a raging ruby burst,
the apple opened a brilliant, seedy grin.
For what more jeweled shining could she thirst?

Now six thousand years she bewails
the lapping copper gleam on the serpent's scales.

A Dream of the Afterlife

I arrived shockingly from nowhere
onto a blazing green lawn where
Dad was cutting the grass.
The elms stood massively symmetrical again,
and the giant oak had sprung up
from its lightning-blasted trunk.
Mom, round-armed and strong
in a crisp dress from sixty years ago
watered the geraniums. The house
stood with shining windows
behind pink rhododendrons,
and inside someone was playing a Chopin waltz
on a perfectly tuned piano.
It might have been Grandpa.
Lilacs and tulips bloomed
beside asters and chrysanthemums.
The sky arched midsummer afternoon blue,
yet fireflies jigged like yellow and green stars
through the sunlight.
Then I knew.

I knew that when
my brother Dale walked smiling up the driveway,

both his legs would have equal strength.
I knew that my Aunt Dolores would rise
smoothly from the picnic bench,
and Grandma would easily
bend her spine to sniff a rose.
I knew that my dimpled, youthful sister Kay
and I had been given two more octaves
to our voices and that
we would sing together again.

I didn't check to see
if my hair was still sparse and white.
There was no need.

Last Lent

This is my eightieth Lent,
and the music moves more
somberly than before. There
are still the hymns and *Glorias*
that pull me closer to God,
drawing me nearer every day
as my long, beautiful life
soars closer to the stars . . .
perhaps only ten Lents left
before I kneel and sing
that last, most glorious
Agnus Dei.

www.ingramcontent.com/pod-product-compliance
Lightning Source LLC
Chambersburg PA
CBHW061251040426
42444CB00010B/2355